DATE DUE

WINSLOW HOMER

BY

FORBES WATSON

Photo Research and Bibliography by

AIMÉE CRANE

NEW YORK
CROWN PUBLISHERS

AMERICAN ARTISTS SERIES
Uniform with this volume

GEORGE BELLOWS, by Peyton Boswell, Jr.
WINSLOW HOMER, by Forbes Watson
THOMAS EAKINS, by Roland McKinney
WHISTLER, by James W. Lane

Other titles in preparation

Contents

Index and List of Illustrations

The pictures listed in italics are in color

I HAVE SPENT summers walking and scrambling over the rocky shores of Maine. Like countless others I have felt the power and grandeur of the Maine coast and watched the huge seas roll in and roar upon the rocks. But I saw it all better after I knew Winslow Homer's paintings. Homer's family had been going to Prout's Neck in the summers since 1875. When he decided to settle there in 1884 and began the series of paintings of surf and rocks, with and without figures, by which he is best known he little knew that some day the coast of New England from one end to the other would become a chain of artists' colonies. It happens in every country. Let an artist make a place famous and other artists will find their way to it. Homer made sea pictures so popular in America that for years after his death seascape specialists, some of them as able as they were imitative, were constantly running away with prizes at the academies. But Homer himself was no specialist. An abundant sense of varied life was projected in his case by a many-faceted output which covered the fields of illustration, watercolor painting and oil painting. Far from limiting himself to the seacoast of Maine, he went to various parts of our country as well as to the West Indies and Canada and his first deep interest in the sea and the life of sailors and fishermen began when he spent two years in Tynemouth, England.

Before discussing further the quality in Homer's art which brought popular success and led him by natural processes of growth to a permanent position of distinction in the annals of American painting, let us glance at his antecedents and at the main events of his life. William Howe Downes, in his *Life and Works of Winslow Homer*, says that the Homer family had been settled in New England since the middle of the seventeenth century. The painter's father, Charles Savage Homer, was a hardware merchant in Boston and his mother, Henrietta Maria Benson, came from Bucksport, Maine. She is said to have had "a pretty talent for painting flowers in watercolors." Winslow himself piously kept his mother's studies. One of them was shown at the Whitney Museum exhibition of American watercolors. A charming and understanding flower painting, with a delicate feeling of growth, it suggested that the son may have inherited from his mother a sense of the real and the unforced. It is not hard to imagine how greatly the mother's watercolors would now be treasured by the ever-growing army of Americana seekers.

The Homer family lived in Boston at the time that Winslow Homer was born, February 24th, 1836. When he was six years old the family moved to Cambridge, which was then a small town. There he enjoyed the life of a country boy and developed the love of the outdoors which never left him. He took up drawing spontaneously as a boy in Cambridge, which had not yet heard the dogmas of Ruskin religiously spread by Charles Eliot Norton, nor yet dreamed that someday it would house a Fogg Museum and send throughout America its meticulous historians of art. But Harvard gave the keynote to the pleasant town and among Homer's first illustrations for *Ballou's Pictorial* was a series called *Life at Harvard*.

He received no special teaching but his early drawings, in their vigor, shrewd observation and instinctive sense of composition, were unmistakable evidence of his natural aptitude. Throughout his entire career Homer developed under circumstances unlike those which appeal to more romantic, less hardy souls. To begin with, his family did not object to his becoming an artist. Then, instead of making the pilgrimage to Europe for "atmosphere" and study which was already an accepted tradition for American artists and which finally, up to this war, was to be considered a necessity, Homer at the age of nineteen went to work for a Boston lithographer named Bufford. There he made a series of titles for sheet music and of portraits of the Massachusetts Senate. After two years he left Bufford and set up for himself, making drawings not only for *Ballou's Pictorial* but for Harper Brothers in New York. In 1859 he left Boston and went to New York and two years later took a studio in the old University Building on Washington Square. Homer did study for a short time in the night class of the National Academy and he took a few "lessons in painting" from a certain Frédéric Rondel who, as Samuel Isham puts it, "taught him how to set a palette and use his brushes." The shortness of his period of formal training would seem to indicate that Homer was not built of the stuff that makes perennial art students.

For almost seventeen years he contributed drawings to Harper's. They covered an immense range of subjects. Genre compositions, often of many figures in black and white, they were subject to a cruder process of reproduction than we use today. Isham suggests that when he went to the Civil War as correspondent for *Harper's Weekly* his sketches had to be "indestructably clear" to withstand the clumsy way in which they were transferred to the wood block. While he was in Washington he drew Lincoln's inauguration and a series of war subjects. It is characteristic that the war pictures were not of heroic battle scenes. There was never any bombast about Homer. His chosen subjects were, rather, episodes in the daily lives of the soldiers—realistic, natural and direct. Meanwhile continuing his work in black and white, he decided to become a painter.

By this time, although he was not thirty, he was known to a wide public through his drawings and when he began to develop his own kind of genre paintings, real subjects presented with sanity, directness and penetration, it was not as an unknown beginner. The earliest paintings were episodes of the Civil War and some of the titles given to these illustrative paintings were: *The Sharpshooter on Picket Duty, Rations, In Front of the Guard House* and *Prisoners From the Front.*

We might note that the tradition of reality which makes Homer's records of the Civil War among our most prized possessions is being followed by the painters who today are beginning to make the pictorial record of this war with its infinitely more destructive weapons. Homer never dreamed of a raid of a thousand planes but the hearts of courage that now fly through the sky were equalled in the breasts of the men who fought at Gettysburg. Homer recognized then, as he would now if he were painting today, that the heart was the essential.

It was part of the natural growth of Homer's genius that he should spend more and more time in the country. He was in search of subjects. But the temporary, casual view of them was not enough for Homer. He had developed a phenomenal visual memory. He was free of esthetic theories and his effort was to convey the intense reality with which the outdoor world and its people, men, and animals, struck him. His harvest included scenes from Negro life, hunting and fishing, and the homely varieties in the life of country people. Since Homer did not look to the art of his predecessors or of his contemporaries for hints of how things should be done he often achieved a quite remarkable originality. He was not in search of subtleties and he was never precious. He sought the truth as he saw it and only as he saw it.

One of the places where he painted before he finally settled by the sea was Hurley, New York, which is near Kingston. Whether the fact that Homer had painted in that region resulted in the neighborhood's becoming a much frequented colony of painters years later is not known. Perhaps Birge Harrison, brother of the more famous Alexander Harrison, knew of Homer's painting there. At any rate, Ulster County is now a center of working artists. Had it been thus when Homer was alive he would probably have sought his subjects elsewhere, for he was always of a solitary disposition, shunning association with other artists, and utterly indifferent to their praise or blame.

One of the curious facts in the history of American painting during the past half century is that although it has been rife with movements that have excited one generation after another, the individuals who have stood out and lasted have been curiously immune to the theories of art which dominated the great mass of their fellow painters. Ryder, Homer, and Eakins all developed their individual styles with a strange disregard of the esthetic activities which affected so many of their contemporaries. Winslow Homer died in Prout's Neck September 29th, 1910 at the age of seventy-four. Thomas Eakins died in 1916 and Albert Ryder in 1917. A whole mass of painters who had been influenced by Barbizon had been succeeded by another mass influenced by the French impressionists, but Homer, Eakins and Ryder, each taking their different paths of development, proceeded as if completely unaware of any such transitions.

Homer's early paintings are all story-telling pictures. Perhaps the only time when any cloud cast its shadow over his reputation as a leader in American painting was during the period when the idea of a "story" in a picture was held in horror by the majority of artists. I can remember talking with a lady, who had studied with Matisse, on her return from France in the year 1912. She sniffed audibly at the idea that a realistic painter of outdoor scenes and people could be held in such high esteem as Homer. For her it was just another proof of our provincialism. In that particular time, when we were taking our first enthusiastic dash into the purest, esthetic realms of abstractionism, the slightest literary content was all that was needed to condemn a painter. Yet a picture can be good or bad with or without a story. Certainly if the artists had been consistent in their repudiation of all art that has content or allusion beyond the limits of painting quality, pure and simple, they would have had to reject much of the world's greatest art. Nearly all the Italian primitives, as well as Michelangelo, Rembrandt, and countless other great artists, contradict the story-telling phobia. It is not the story that can make a story picture bad; it is the triviality of the painting in it.

The work of this part of Homer's life marks a definite and significant stage in his development as an artist. In quality of painting the pictures are somewhat meagre, in color of no great richness. Human interest they have always had for the average observer, and the more discerning eye will recognize the unconventional quality of observa-

tion in them, their unforced and unaffected truth. Affectation or false-
ness of any kind is unthinkable in connection with Winslow Homer.
Incidentally, this group of his genre paintings, descriptive paintings
if you like, provides a unique record of the social history of our country
from the 'sixties to the 'eighties.

But if Homer's work had stopped at this time, or had developed no
further, he would by no means have held the high place in American
art that he holds today. He was a man of slow growth, in spite of his
prodigious production, and his later years brought a vast increase in
breadth and power. To follow the course of any strong painter's
evolution is to watch him grow in the capacity to select the important
and eliminate the unimportant. With the dropping of each non-
essential the form becomes more abstract and consequently more real.
We may say that it is not the transitory changes in the quality of flesh
that establish a head, but the feeling for the skeleton which the artist
recognizes beneath the passing changes. That may be why pure in-
vention can never be quite as abstract as the underlying foundation of
a reality.

According to Homer himself, he merely tried to paint the thing he
saw as truly as he could. The esthetic pretensions which flower under
the artificial sun of publicity, the theories that are made of words and
sound so fine in language, were unknown to Homer. At the age of
nineteen he said that, "If a man wants to be an artist he must never
look at pictures." But this dogma did not rule Homer's life. Though
he apparently paid little attention to the works of his contemporaries,
while receiving their acclaim, he was quietly well enough aware of
them to decide who were genuine and who were makers of potboilers.
I have this story from a dealer in whose back room Homer occasionally
visited. While he was there one day another painter came in, one of

those men who manufactured over and over the one picture that had been his best seller. He caught a glimpse of Homer and asked the dealer if he would not do him the honor of introducing him to the great man. When the dealer conveyed the request to Homer, the reply was: "Tell Mr. G—— to go to hell."

This is not the remark of an artist who never looked at other men's pictures. Although Homer may be said to have conquered the public and won the high esteem of his fellow artists, it was not through any effort on his part to swerve, for popularity's sake, from the line of truth as he saw it. He concentrated on developing his intensely individual point of view from the sources of life rather than from the sources of art. One painter will say that, "It is in the museums that you learn about art"; another will say that, "We should burn up the museums and free the creative artist of today from the burden of the past"; and still another will sneer that the museums are good enough for laymen or historians but that the true artist should turn his back on them and go to nature. Any one of these statements, which have been made many times, has a babe-and-suckling quality, but is not necessarily wisdom. Yet every one of them, like other declarations by artists, is indicative of a strength or a weakness. Perhaps it would be truer to say that they indicate, each in its own way, limitations.

Conceivably the wise artist knows his limitations and his needs. The late Charles Demuth, speaking of John Marin, once said to me: "I get my inspiration from the same source as Marin, but I get mine in a teaspoon and never spill a drop, and he gets his in a pail and spills it all over the place." Homer did not get his inspiration either in a teaspoon or in a pail. He found it in the ocean beating with tremendous power upon the rocks. He found it in men's struggles with the elements of sea and land. He found it in palm trees bending in tropical breezes, in Civil War characters, in camp fires, in school children playing Snap the Whip, in ladies playing croquet, in wrecks and life-savers, in animals and fish, and sailors and storms. Always he found it in life, in the many realities which his extraordinarily observing eyes took in during a strong and healthy productive period, throughout which he used a plain language which could be understood by plain people.

Homer died five years before the thirty-year war of eclecticism which began in Paris in 1911 and which was enjoying an esthetic boudoir reincarnation when the first shots were heard in Pearl Harbor. Doubtless he lived at the right time for himself and his ideas. It was a good period in which a strong native painter could develop his ideas in America. It has been said that all strong painters are national in feeling and that the strongest of them are international in scope. If we compare Homer as a painter with Lincoln as a prose writer, or Whitman as a poet, we may be led to wonder whether it was not the writers who penetrated further beyond the boundaries of their country than the healthy, tangy, virile and national Homer.

Homer had been exhibiting his episodic pictures at the National Academy exhibitions, first in the galleries known as the Institute of Art, 625 Broadway, and later at the new building at the corner of Fourth Avenue and 23rd Street. The paintings had some success from the first, and Homer was made an Associate of the Academy in 1864, and a member in the following year, being still under thirty years of age. In spite of his reticences and coldness toward other artists' work, Homer never had reason to complain of any lack of recognition from them. From his earlier quarters in Washington Square, Homer now moved to the old studio building on West 10th Street where so many artists have worked. LaFarge also had a studio in the same building and the two artists were acquainted, apparently not intimately, although LaFarge thought highly of Homer's work. Among his other friends were R. M. Shurtleff, Homer Martin, John F. Weir, Alfred C. Howland and William M. Chase.

As we have seen, Homer wandered over New York State, New England and Virginia in search of subjects and now, in 1867, he went to Europe. He did a few drawings for *Harper's Weekly—Dancing at Mabille, Dancing at the Casino,* and *Artists and Copyists* in the Louvre. During the two months spent in France he did no painting for himself, joined no classes and associated with no artists. Assuming that he went to the galleries, no evidence of outside influence entered his own work as a result.

The watercolors began to appear in the early 'seventies. At first they were really drawings with watercolor added. Though done with his usual precision and truth, they are a long way from the magnificent breadth and force he afterwards achieved in that medium. Some illustrate the pursuits of children in the country. Later subjects were found about Gloucester Harbor. A group of these was exhibited in Boston in 1878, and the public showed themselves eager to buy, at prices ranging from seventy-five to a hundred dollars. From this time on the watercolors became more numerous in his output, gaining steadily in design and vigor of statement. The long years of patient observation were bearing fruit.

In those days the interior decorator had not been invented and the steamroller of art publicity had not been developed. Nice people bought paintings and hung them in their parlors, their dining rooms and front halls. They were prosperous, sound people and the paintings, hung in crowded disarray, were bought because they were liked and supplied an innocent enough proof of solidity and cultivation.

The international collector had not yet appeared. The intense pressure of name-making, taught to us by Paris, had not begun. For better or for worse, people naïvely bought pictures because they liked them. They liked the American landscape, preferably in a romantic mood. They liked the stormy seas and paintings which brought thoughts of brave adventure into their parlors. The main point is, I think, that they liked their pictures. They did not buy great pictures by great names simply because they thought they ought to like them or because they would add "importance" to their collections.

We have long forgotten such childlike reactions in our days of sophistication, but apparently when Homer painted, the affection which people had for his work was not unpleasant to him. I was told by one of Homer's friends that on one occasion a lady wrote to him that her husband was dying of consumption and that his greatest desire was to have on his sickroom wall, during the too short remainder of his life, some paintings by Winslow Homer. "He loves your pictures but cannot afford to buy them," the lady wrote to Homer. Homer shipped some pictures and they were duly hung, to the delight of the dying man. When the man died, the widow wrote to Homer, thanked him again for the pictures and asked him where she should send them. Homer, the solitary and unsociable, wrote to her that people who loved his pictures so much must have his pictures and begged her to keep them for herself. It is a hearsay story but for my part I believe it. It was the same Homer who sent word to "Mr. G——" to go to hell and the stories seem to me completely consistent. It has been my experience that artists who are enraged by fake painting are more human than those who are ever tactful.

After Homer settled at Prout's Neck his patient and penetrating observation and his extraordinary memory of visual impressions began to bear their richest fruit. His sense of force, movement and volume, always acute, was extended to its utmost in the canvases that he painted of the conflict of sea and rocky shore. In these subjects and in this type of descriptive painting he stands alone. He often spent whole days looking at the sea without touching a brush. Although, once having begun, he worked with the greatest ardor, he sometimes waited for weeks for the conditions he wanted. He was not being romantic and waiting for inspiration. He had his picture in mind and was waiting for nature to supply the model. To make his constant study of the sea and weather more satisfactory he had a little painting-house made on runners with a big plate glass window. This could be moved to the chosen spot, giving him shelter from the weather as well as protection from inquisitive visitors, always his chief aversion. Though so different in character from Cézanne, Homer's attitude toward people, and toward the ladies in particular, often suggests the peculiarities of the master of Aix.

Meanwhile, Homer's reputation was steadily growing. The amount of his production may be judged from the fact that he was able to hold, usually, two exhibitions a year in Boston where his popular success was won earlier than in New York. The market was good, recognition was liberal, his pictures were in demand by dealers and museums and by the non-professional public. His success was natural and was based on the appeal that his pictures made to people in general. It was not a manipulated success, not a manufactured fame. The "Gulf Stream" was acquired by the Metropolitan Museum in New York from the Chicago World's Fair in 1893. Homer exhibited fifteen canvases and was awarded a gold medal.

For the remainder of his active painting life he won numerous honors, and if his misanthropic tendencies increased with age it was through no want of appreciation. Every museum in the country was anxious to get his pictures. The years which saw this series of triumphs for his marine paintings also brought forth what, to my mind, is the finest work of his life—namely, the later watercolors. Leaving Prout's Neck during the coldest of the winter months for the Bahama Islands, Cuba, and Florida, Homer found keen stimulus in the semi-tropical scene. He produced with amazing fertility the brilliant series of watercolors which possibly may hold his fame more permanently than his imposing big canvases. These later watercolors differ greatly from his earlier more tentative works in the same medium. Of these watercolors Homer himself said that they were "as good work, with the exception of one or two etchings, as I ever did." For intensity, direct and powerful statement, luminosity and trenchant economy of means, they are unsurpassed.

It is evident that Winslow Homer had the good fortune to find more complete fulfillment of his natural gifts than it falls to the lot of most men to attain. One field in which also he might possibly have succeeded remained almost unexplored—that of mural painting, the field in which the American painters of the past ten years have made, thanks to the enterprise of their Government, the most important contribution to our art that any single decade has seen. It is on record that Homer did receive a commission to paint on the wall of Harper and Brothers office and that he applied to LaFarge for advice. In a letter to Gustav Kobbe, LaFarge stated that he had seen the project for such a decoration and that "it was as learned as if this man had consulted all the necessary books." Inadvertently this quotation contains all the reasons why so much American mural decoration, from the time of the Chicago Fair of 1893 through the completion of the Library of Congress and the Boston Public Library, looks like a lifeless scrapbook blown upon the wall. At the time when the Boston Library decorations were being planned, St. Gaudens wrote to the architect, McKim, proposing names of painters to be commissioned for the work. Winslow Homer's name was included in the list with the remark that Abbey had said that Homer had done "some bully decorative things in Harper's office." This information I have culled from Downes' Life of Homer and Mr. Downes goes on to say that on hearing of the existence of the work he "called at Harper and Bros. establishment, February, 1911, and asked about these decorations, but nobody knew anything about them, and though a frieze in the office was shown, it apparently did not include the panels by Homer."

One cannot but speculate as to how Homer would have met the problems of the mural painter. He certainly was not what is known as a "decorative painter" and, considering his strong bent toward realism, it is difficult to imagine him seeing anything he might paint as a part of a wall and of a room rather than as a live entity existing in and for itself. But his design was strong and he certainly could have done something more enlivening than the kind of experienced mural painter who too timidly and conscientiously accepts the architect's dogma on the correct subordination of the mural to the room. As LaFarge said, he painted his apparently unique mural commission as if he had "consulted all the necessary books." And the fact that he probably didn't consult them may have enabled him to escape the dilution of vigor which too much consulting sometimes brings about. In this connection we might recall his youthful brash statement that "if a man wants to be an artist he must never look at pictures."

With the approach of age Homer became more and more of a recluse, receiving ungraciously even the sincerest homage and using a rubber stamp of his name in reply to requests for his autograph. But occasionally some of the younger painters who had already begun to flock to Maine in his wake did break down his seclusion and after the first crustiness the old painter sometimes examined and reviewed their work sympathetically. But this was evidently so rare an event that the artists who enjoyed it still talk about it as an underlined reminiscence. It is probable that the reticence and exclusiveness which was a marked trait of his character all his life was a form of instinctive self-protection from distraction and interruptions. He was certainly as jealous of his independence as Cézanne. That he sometimes felt, in rejecting the human companionship that most men need, he was missing one of the great sources of happiness, is indicated by his saying on one occasion to Mrs. Joseph De Camp that one of the mistakes of his life was that he did not affiliate himself "with the boys," meaning the painters.

He fell into periods of despondency, and declared from time to time his intention to quit painting for good, a decision to which he did not consistently adhere. Probably he was aware of declining powers and loathed the idea of producing work inferior to his best. He had a serious illness in 1908 from which he only partially recovered. After that he painted a few watercolors and his last oil painting, *Driftwood*. He died, as already noted, at Prout's Neck, September 29th, 1910, at the age of seventy-four.

In reviewing the story of Winslow Homer's work the outstanding trait is that most important of gifts for the painter—creative vitality. He painted without suavity, usually without charm. His great distinction lay in his power and freedom; his great good fortune was the unlimited abundance of his energy. Those artists who can manage to squeeze out just enough for the work in hand will always look like weaklings beside him. In art enough is not enough.

SELECTED BIBLIOGRAPHY

WINSLOW HOMER

Born Boston 1836
Died Prout's Neck 1910

He studied in America and received a most informal art training. Was a correspondent for "Harper's Weekly" 1858-76. Started to paint in 1876 (40 years old). Visited Canada, Adirondacks, the Bahamas, Florida, Cuba and Bermuda.

BOOKS ON HOMER

NATHANIEL POUSETTE-DART, *Winslow Homer*. New York, 1923, Frederick A. Stokes Co.

KENYON COX, *Winslow Homer*. New York, 1914, privately printed by F. F. Sherman.

WILLIAM HOWE DOWNES, *Life and Works of Winslow Homer*. Boston and New York, 1911, Houghton, Mifflin & Co.

Books-General

Holger Cahill and Alfred H. Barr, Jr., ed., *Art in America in Modern Times*. New York, 1934, Reynal & Hitchcock.

Frank Jewett Mather, Jr., *Estimates in Art*. New York, 1931, Henry Holt & Co.

Lewis Mumford, *The Brown Decades*. New York, 1931, Harcourt Brace & Co.

Suzanne La Follette, *Art in America*. New York, 1929, Harper Bros.

Duncan Phillips, *Brief Estimates of the Painters in A Collection in the Making*. New York, 1926, Phillips Publications, No. 5, E. Weyhe.

Royal Cortissoz, *American Artists*. New York, 1923, Charles Scribner's Sons.

A. E. Gallatin, *American Watercolourists*. New York, 1922, E. P. Dutton & Co.

Frederic Fairchild Sherman, *American Painters of Yesterday and Today*. New York, 1919, privately printed.

Frederic Fairchild Sherman, *Landscape and Figure Painting*. New York, 1917.

Charles Henry Caffin, *Story of American Painting*. New York, 1907, Frederick A. Stokes Co.

Samuel Isham, *The History of American Painting*. New York, 1905 and 1927, Macmillan Co.

Charles Henry Caffin, *American Masters of Painting*. New York, 1902, Doubleday, Page & Co.

Sadakichi Hartmann, *History of American Art*. Boston, 1902, L. C. Page & Co.

William Howe Downes, *Twelve Great Artists*. Boston, 1900, Little, Brown & Co.

Mrs. M. G. Van Rensselaer, *Six Portraits*. Boston and New York, 1889, Houghton, Mifflin & Co.

GEORGE WILLIAM SHELDON, *American Painters*. New York, 1879, D. Appleton & Co.

EDWARD STRAHAN, *The Art Treasures of America*. Philadelphia, 1879, George Barrie.

EXHIBITION CATALOGUES

LIVING AMERICAN ART, New York. *Winslow Homer,* 1940. By Robert W. Macbeth.

WHITNEY MUSEUM OF AMERICAN ART, New York. *Winslow Homer, Centenary Exhibition,* 1937. Foreword by Lloyd Goodrich.

NEW ENGLAND MUSEUMS ASSOCIATION. *Winslow Homer, Watercolors, Prints and Drawings,* 1936.

PROUT'S NECK ASSOCIATION, Prout's Neck, Maine. *Century Loan Exhibition,* 1936. Foreword by Robert W. Macbeth.

MUSEUM OF MODERN ART, New York. *Homer—Ryder—Eakins Exhibition,* 1930. Foreword by Frank Jewett Mather, Jr.

CARNEGIE INSTITUTE, Pittsburgh. *Watercolors by Winslow Homer,* 1923. Foreword by Royal Cortissoz.

CARNEGIE INSTITUTE, Pittsburgh. *Watercolors by Homer and Sargent,* 1917.

BROOKLYN MUSEUM, New York, *Watercolors by Winslow Homer,* 1915. Foreword by William H. Goodyear.

METROPOLITAN MUSEUM OF ART, New York. *Winslow Homer Memorial Exhibition,* 1911.

PERIODICALS

WORCESTER ART MUSEUM ANNUAL, 1937-1938. *A Lost Winslow Homer,* by Lloyd Goodrich.

COMMONWEAL, April, 1936. *Winslow Homer Artist,* by James W. Lane.

ART NEWS, May 1936. *Winslow Homer: Oils, Watercolors and Drawings in a Centenary Exhibit Current in Philadelphia,* by Henry Clifford.

ART DIGEST, August 1936. *Homer, Artist and Man, Revealed at Show in His Old Studio.*

BULLETIN OF THE NEW YORK PUBLIC LIBRARY, Oct. 1936. *Check List of Illustrations by Winslow Homer,* by Allen Evarts Foster.

AMERICAN MAGAZINE OF ART, Oct. 1936. *Winslow Homer,* by Forbes Watson.

AMERICAN MAGAZINE OF ART, July 1935. *Winslow Homer's Early Illustrations,* by Allen Weller.

ART IN AMERICA, March 1934. *A Note on Winslow Homer's Drawings in Harper's Weekly,* by Allen Weller.

HOUND & HORN, July-Sept. 1933. *Remington and Winslow Homer,* by John Wheelwright.

BULLETIN OF THE NEW YORK PUBLIC LIBRARY, Nov. 1932. *Winslow Homer and the Woodblock,* by Frank Weitenkampf.

FINE ARTS, April 1932. *Watercolors by Homer—Critique and Catalogue,* by Theodore Bolton.

FINE ARTS, Feb. 1932. *The Art of Winslow Homer: An Estimate in 1932,* by Theodore Bolton.

AMERICAN MAGAZINE OF ART, Nov. 1931. *American Painters of the Sea,* by William Howe Downes.

ART IN AMERICA, Dec. 1930. *Winslow Homer's Drawings in Harper's Weekly,* by E. P. Richardson.

ARTS, May 1930. *Ryder, Eakins, Homer. Museum of Modern Art Exhibition,* by Forbes Watson.

THE ARTS, Oct. 1924. *Winslow Homer,* by Lloyd Goodrich.

BULLETIN OF THE METROPOLITAN MUSEUM OF ART, Feb. 1923. *Early Paintings by Homer,* by Harry B. Wehle.

THE FORUM, Dec. 1915. *Modern American Painters—and Winslow Homer,* by Willard Huntington Wright.

BROOKLYN MUSEUM QUARTERLY, Oct. 1915. *Winslow Homer,* by William H. Goodyear.

L'Art et les Artistes, Oct. 1912-Mar. 1913. *Winslow Homer et la signification de son oeuvre,* by Walter Pach.

Nation, March 1911. *Art of Winslow Homer,* by Frank Jewett Mather, Jr.

World's Work, Feb. 1911. *Winslow Homer, a Painter of the Sea,* by Arthur Hoeber.

Scribner's Magazine, Jan. 1911. *Winslow Homer,* by Christian Brinton.

Harper's Weekly, Oct. 1910. *Some Recollections of Winslow Homer,* by J. Eastman Chase.

International Studio, June 1908. *Winslow Homer,* by Leila Mechlin.

Brush and Pencil, 1902. *Winslow Homer, Artist,* by Frederic W. Morton.

Our Young Folks, July 1866. *Among the Studios,* by Thomas Bailey Aldrich.

WINSLOW HOMER

The Conch Divers   *Watercolor*   1885
14″ x 20″
Collection of The Minneapolis Institute of Arts

A Sunday Morning in Virginia   *Oil*   1877
18″ x 24″
Collection Cincinnati Art Museum

Right:
Palm Tree, Nassau   *Watercolor*   1898
23⅛″ x 15″
Collection Metropolitan Museum of Art, New York

Return from the Hunt   *Watercolor*   1892
18¾″ x 24¾″
Collection Los Angeles Museum of History, Science and Art

Honossasa Jungle in Florida
Watercolor   1904
14″ x 21½″
Courtesy of the Fogg Museum of Art,
Harvard University

Right:
Herring Net   *Oil*   1885
30″ x 48″
Courtesy of The Art Institute of Chic
Colorplate: Courtesy of Simon and S

Croquet Players   *Oil*   1865
16″ x 26″
Collection of the Albright Art Gallery, Buffalo

Study of a Soldier   *Drawing*   1883
13¼″ x 8¼″
Collection Cincinnati Art Museum

A Rainy Day in Camp   *Oil*   1871
19⅞" x 36"
Collection Metropolitan Museum of Art, New York

Drawing   *Crayon*   1863
14" x 9"
Courtesy of The Cooper Union Museum for the Arts of Decoration

Drawing   *Charcoal and Crayon*   1865
17″ x 15″
Courtesy of The Cooper Union Museum for the Arts of Decoration

After the Tornado, Bahamas   *Watercolor*   c. 1898
14½" x 21"
Courtesy of The Art Institute of Chicago

Sloop, Bermuda
Watercolor   1899
15″ x 21½″
Collection
Metropolitan
Museum of Art,
New York

The Bather
Watercolor   1899
14¼″ x 21″
Collection
Metropolitan
Museum of Art,
New York

Gathering Autumn Leaves   *Oil*   c. 1873
38¼″ x 24¼″
Courtesy of The Cooper Union Museum for the Arts of Decoration

A Country Lad   *Oil*   1873
22¾" x 15½"
Courtesy of The Cooper Union Museum for the Arts of Decoration

The Bridlepath, White Mountains   *Oil*   1868
24″ x 38″
Collection of the Whitney Museum of American Art, New York

Pumpkin Patch   *Watercolor*   1878
11½″ x 19⅞″
Courtesy of the Ferargil Galleries, New York

The Lookout   *Watercolor*   1882
4¼" x 21¼"
Courtesy of the Fogg Museum of Art, Harvard University

Left:
Moonlight, Wood's Island Light   *Oil*   1894
0¾" x 40¼"
Collection Metropolitan Museum of Art, New York

The Watermelon Boys   *Oil*   1876
38½" x 24"
Courtesy of The Cooper Union Museum for the Arts of Decoration

ew England Country School   *Oil*   1873
2″ x 18″
ollection of the Addison Gallery of American Art, Phillips Academy, Andover

da
color

x 20½″
sy of the
lphia
m of Art,
lphia

On the Beach   *Oil*   1878
25" x 18½"
From the Chester Dale Collection, New York

The Croquet Players
Black Chalk   1866
11⅝″ x 10″
Collection Metropolitan Museum of Art,
New York

The Life Line   *Drawing*   1882-83
17 4/5″ x 15 1/5″
Courtesy of The Cooper Union Museum for the Arts of Decoration

The Life Line   *Oil*   1884
30″ x 44″
Courtesy of the Philadelphia Museum of Art, Philadelphia

The Signal of Distress   *Drawing*   c. 1890
14″ x 11 4/5″
Courtesy of The Cooper Union Museum for the Arts of Decoration

Defiance: Inviting a Shot Before Petersburg, Va.   *Oil*   1864
12″ x 18″
Collection of the Whitney Museum of American Art, New York

Pitching Quoits   *Oil*
26″ x 53¼″
Courtesy of the Fogg Museum of Art,
Harvard University

The Wreck   *Oil*   1896
30" x 48"
Courtesy of Carnegie Institute, Pittsburgh

Left:
Searchlight, Harbor Entrance, Santiago de Cuba   *Oil*   1901
30⅝" x 50½"
Collection Metropolitan Museum of Art, New York

Drawing   *Pencil and Pen-and-ink*   1867
11″ x 7″
Courtesy of The Cooper Union Museum for the Arts of Decoration

Drawing   *Crayon*   1863
14″ x 8″
Courtesy of The Cooper Union Museum for the Arts of Decoration

Drawing   *Charcoal and Crayon*   c. 1864
25" x 16"
Courtesy of The Cooper Union Museum for the Arts of Decoration

Homer

25.165

A Fisher G[irl]
on the Beac[h]
Drawing
c. 1881
14¾" x 11⅜[?]
Collection
Metropolita[n]
Museum of [Art]
New York

On the Beach   *Drawing*   1884
15½″ x 23½″
Courtesy of the Babcock Galleries, New York

Children Playing Under
a Gloucester Wharf
Watercolor   1880
8″ x 13¼″
Courtesy Museum of
Fine Arts, Boston

A Light on the Sea   *Oil*   1897
28″ x 48″
Collection of The Corcoran Gallery of Art, Washington, D. C.

Eastern Point   *Oil*   1900
30″ x 48″
Collection of the Addison Gallery
of American Art,
Phillips Academy, Andover

Hauling in Anchor, Key West   *Watercolor*
13½″ x 21½″
Collection Cincinnati Art Museum

awing
ayon   c. 1881-82
″ x 7″

urtesy of
e Cooper Union
seum for the
ts of Decoration

Street Scene, Santiago de Cuba   *Watercolor*   1885
11¾" x 17¼"
Courtesy of the Philadelphia Museum of Art, Philadelphia

Right:
Fresh Air   *Watercolor*   1878
20¼" x 13¾"
In the Collection of the Brooklyn Museum, New York

Croquet Scene   *Oil*   1866
16" x 26"
Courtesy of The Art Institute of Chicago

Under the Cocoanut Palm   *Watercolor*   1890
14⅝″ x 20⅞″
Courtesy of the Fogg Museum of Art, Harvard University

Right:
Spanish Flag, Santiago de Cuba   *Watercolor*   1885
12¼″ x 16¼″
Courtesy of the Philadelphia Museum of Art, Philadelphia

Fisher Folk in Dory   *Watercolor*   1881
13¼" x 19"
Courtesy of the Fogg Museum of Art, Harvard University

Right:
Northeaster   *Oil*   1895
34⅜" x 50¼"
Collection Metropolitan
Museum of Art, New York

The Last Boat In
Crayon Drawing   1885
8" x 12"
Collection of the Addison
Gallery of American Art,
Phillips Academy, Andover

adian Camp, Montagnais Indians, Quebec   *Watercolor*   1895
3½" x 19¾"
ourtesy Museum of Fine Arts, Boston

HOMER
1876

Flower Garden and Bungalow, Bermuda   *Watercolor*   1899
14″ x 21″
Collection Metropolitan Museum of Art, New York

Left:
The Lookout—All's Well   *Oil*   1896
40⅛″ x 30¼″
Courtesy Museum of Fine Arts, Boston

The Wrecked Schooner
Watercolor   c. 1909
15″ x 21½″
Collection City Art Museum, St. Louis

North Woods   *Chromo-lithograph*
14½" x 21"
Collection of the Addison Gallery of American Art, Phillips Academy, Andover

Pike, Lake St. John
Watercolor   1897
13¾" x 20⅝"
Courtesy of the
Fogg Museum of
Art,
Harvard University

The Gale   *Oil*   1893
32" x 48"
Collection Worcester Art Museum

The Dory   *Watercolor*   c. 1887
33⅜" x 20½"
Courtesy Museum of Fine Arts,
Boston

Drawing   *Charcoal*   c. 1878
22 2/5″ x 14″
Courtesy of The Cooper Union Museum for the Arts of Decoration

Waverly Oaks   *Drawing*   c. 1875
8″ x 6″
Courtesy of The Cooper Union Museum
for the Arts of Decoration

Two Young Girls   *Drawing*   c. 1878
10½″ x 7″
Courtesy of The Cooper Union Museum for the Arts of Decoration

Promenade on the Bea[ch]
Oil   1880
19½″ x 29″
Collection of
The Springfield Muse[um]
of Fine Arts

Girls with Lobster
Watercolor   c. 187[9]
9″ x 13⅜″
Courtesy of the
Macbeth Gallery,
New York

Drawing   *Charcoal*   c. 1863
17" x 10"
Courtesy of The Cooper Union Museum for the Arts of Decoration

Right and Left   *Oil*   1909
28⅜″ x 48½″
Collection of Mrs. Randal Morgan, Philadelphia

Man with a Knapsack   *Oil*   1873
22½" x 15¼"
Courtesy of The Cooper Union Museum for the Arts of Decoration

Left:
The Fox Hunt   *Oil*   1893
38" x 68"
Collection of The Pennsylvania Academy of the Fine Arts, Philadelphia

The Hare Hunt   *Oil*   1882
15⅜″ x 28⅛″
Collection of Mr. and Mrs. Jacob H. Rand, New York

Edge of the Farm   *Pencil Drawing*   c. 1875
9½″ x 13½″
Courtesy of Goodman-Walker, Inc., Boston

Haymaking   *Oil*   1864
16″ x 11″
Collection of The Columbus Gallery of Fine Arts

Drawing   *Charcoal*   c. 1881
11¾" x 8"
Courtesy of The Cooper Union Museum for the Arts of Decoration

Returning Fishing Boats   *Watercolor*   1883
15¾" x 24¾"
Courtesy of the Fogg Museum of Art, Harvard University

The Bathers   *Charcoal and White Chalk*   1882
5⁄8″ x 19¾″
ollection Metropolitan Museum of Art, New York

Haul of Herring
rawing   1884
⅞″ x 23 5⁄16″
urtesy Museum of Fine Arts,
oston

Skating in the Central Park
Winslow Homer

Skating in Central Park   *Watercolor*   1858
16¼″ x 24″
Courtesy of the City Art Museum, St. Louis

Early Evening   *Oil*   1881-1907
33″ x 38¾″
Courtesy of the Freer Gallery of Art, Washington, D. C.

Left:
Fog Warning   *Oil*   1885
30″ x 48″
Courtesy Museum of Fine Arts, Boston

ght Bells   *Oil*   1888
' x 30"
llection of the Addison Gallery of American Art, Phillips Academy, Andover

t:
o Girls on a Cliff   *Wash Drawing*
²" x 14"
rtesy of the Fogg Museum of Art, Harvard University

Negro Boy with Sunflower   *Watercolor*   1875
7¼" x 5½"
Courtesy of Mrs. A. P. Homer, Virginia Beach

Right: The Carnival   *Oil*   1877
20" x 30"
Collection Metropolitan Museum of Art, New Y

W.H.

Girl with Checker Board   *Wash Drawing*
Collection Cincinnati Art Museum

Amateur Musicians   *Oil*   1867
18″ x 15″
Collection Metropolitan Museum of Art, New York

Hudson River   *Watercolor*   1892
13½″ x 19¾″
Collection Metropolitan Museum of Art, New York

Hudson River—Logging   *Watercolor*   1897
14″ x 21″
Collection of The Corcoran Gallery of Art, Washington, D. C.

Rocky Shore, Bermuda
Watercolor   1900
13½″ x 19¾″
Courtesy Museum of Fine Arts,
Boston

Huntsman and Dogs   *Oil*   1891
28¼" x 48"
Courtesy of the Philadelphia Museum of Art, Philadelphia

naniche Fishing
tercolor   1897
⁄" x 20¾"
rtesy Museum of
e Arts, Boston

Looking Out to Sea   *Oil*
13¼" x 19"
Courtesy of the Fogg Museum of Art, Harvard University

Left:
Return of the Gleaner   *Oil*   1867
24" x 18"
Collection of Stephen C. Clark, New York

Prisoners from the Front   *Oil*   1866
24" x 38"
Collection Metropolitan Museum of Art, New York

Sketch in Front of Yorktown
Pen and Crayon Drawing   1862
8" x 13⅞"
Collection of the Addison Gallery
of American Art,
Phillips Academy, Andover